Copyright © 2022 by Superior Works Publishing, LLC
All rights reserved. No part of this book may be reproduced or used in any manner without written permission of the copyright owner except for the use of quotations in a book review.
First paperback edition August 2022
ISBN 978-1-7370239-9-9 (paperback)
Published by Superior Works Publishing
https://superiorworkspub.com

Your Vision Planner

Having a goal or dream in mind is one thing, but that goal or vision can become a reality when you write it down. This journal is here to help you do just that.

Psychology professor Dr. Gail Matthews completed a study with 267 participants, men, and women of various professions. She had half of them write down their goals, and the other half did not. She discovered that those who wrote down their goals were most likely to achieve them than those who did not write their goals. She also found that one can become 42% more likely to achieve their goals and dreams by writing them down.1

This journal is here to help you take your goals and dreams to the next level. Whether you are setting financial, health, business, or spiritual goals, this journal applies. Use this book as your companion guide. There's space for you to write 100 dreams/goals, track your progress, encourage yourself, and see it through to completion. This journal takes goal setting to the next level.

I hope that this will be a valuable tool in your life.

~Khadijah Robaina
Superior Works Publishing

Footnote:
1. Mary Morrisey. The Power of Writing Down Your Goals and Dreams. *Huff Post*, 2017

| Date: ___/___/___ | Dream/Goal (Write a clear, specific goal): |

How is this dream relevant to your life?

Achieve by (Date): ___/___/_____

Track your progress:

Date	Accomplishments

Trust the process…

Reflect (Lessons Learned):

Encourage yourself:

Date Goal completed:

How will you celebrate?

© Superior Works Publishing 2022

Draw/Plan/Notes:

Date:
____/____/____

Dream/Goal (Write a clear, specific goal):
_____
_____
_____
_____
_____
_____
_____
_____

How is this dream relevant to your life?
_____
_____
_____
_____
_____
_____

Achieve by (Date):
____/____/____

Track your progress:

Date	Accomplishments

Trust the process…

Reflect (Lessons Learned):
_____
_____
_____
_____
_____
_____
_____
_____

Encourage yourself:
_____
_____
_____
_____
_____
_____
_____
_____
_____

Date Goal completed:
_____

How will you celebrate?
_____
_____
_____
_____
_____

© Superior Works Publishing 2022

Draw/Plan/Notes:

Date:	Dream/Goal (Write a clear, specific goal):
___/___/___	_____

How is this dream relevant to your life?
_____
_____
_____
_____
_____
_____

Dream/Goal (Write a clear, specific goal):
_____
_____
_____
_____
_____
_____
_____

Achieve by (Date):
___/___/_____

Track your progress:

Date	Accomplishments

Trust the process...

Reflect (Lessons Learned):
_____
_____
_____
_____
_____
_____
_____
_____

Encourage yourself:
_____
_____
_____
_____
_____
_____
_____
_____
_____
_____

Date Goal completed:
_____

How will you celebrate?
_____
_____
_____
_____
_____

© Superior Works Publishing 2022

Draw/Plan/Notes:

© Superior Works Publishing 2022

Date:
___/___/___

Dream/Goal (Write a clear, specific goal):
_____
_____
_____
_____
_____
_____
_____

How is this dream relevant to your life?
_____
_____
_____
_____
_____

Achieve by (Date):
___/___/_____

Track your progress:

Date	Accomplishments

Trust the process…

Reflect (Lessons Learned):
_____
_____
_____
_____
_____
_____
_____

Encourage yourself:
_____
_____
_____
_____
_____
_____
_____
_____

Date Goal completed:
_____

How will you celebrate?
_____
_____
_____
_____
_____

© Superior Works Publishing 2022

Draw/Plan/Notes:

Date:
____/____/____

Dream/Goal (Write a clear, specific goal):
_____
_____
_____
_____
_____
_____
_____

How is this dream relevant to your life?
_____
_____
_____
_____
_____

Achieve by (Date):
____/____/_____

Track your progress:

Date	Accomplishments

Trust the process…

Reflect (Lessons Learned):
_____
_____
_____
_____
_____
_____
_____
_____
_____

Encourage yourself:
_____
_____
_____
_____
_____
_____
_____
_____
_____
_____

Date Goal completed:
_____

How will you celebrate?
_____
_____
_____
_____
_____

© Superior Works Publishing 2022

Draw/Plan/Notes:

Date:
____/____/____

Dream/Goal (Write a clear, specific goal):
_____
_____
_____
_____
_____
_____
_____

How is this dream relevant to your life?
_____
_____
_____
_____
_____

Achieve by (Date):
____/____/_____

Track your progress:

Date	Accomplishments

Trust the process…

Reflect (Lessons Learned):
_____
_____
_____
_____
_____
_____
_____
_____
_____

Encourage yourself:
_____
_____
_____
_____
_____
_____
_____
_____
_____
_____
_____

Date Goal completed:
_____

How will you celebrate?
_____
_____
_____
_____
_____

© Superior Works Publishing 2022

Draw/Plan/Notes:

Date:
____/____/____

Dream/Goal (Write a clear, specific goal):
_____
_____
_____
_____
_____
_____
_____

How is this dream relevant to your life?
_____
_____
_____
_____
_____
_____

Achieve by (Date):
____/____/_____

Track your progress:

Date	Accomplishments

Trust the process…

Reflect (Lessons Learned):
_____
_____
_____
_____
_____
_____
_____
_____

Encourage yourself:
_____
_____
_____
_____
_____
_____
_____
_____
_____

Date Goal completed:
_____

How will you celebrate?
_____
_____
_____
_____
_____

© Superior Works Publishing 2022

Draw/Plan/Notes:

Date:
____/____/____

How is this dream relevant to your life?
_____
_____
_____
_____
_____

Dream/Goal (Write a clear, specific goal):
_____
_____
_____
_____
_____
_____
_____

Achieve by (Date):
____/____/_____

Track your progress:

Date	Accomplishments

Trust the process…

Reflect (Lessons Learned):
_____
_____
_____
_____
_____
_____
_____
_____

Encourage yourself:
_____
_____
_____
_____
_____
_____
_____
_____
_____

Date Goal completed:
_____

How will you celebrate?
_____
_____
_____
_____
_____

© Superior Works Publishing 2022

Draw/Plan/Notes:

Date:
___/___/___

Dream/Goal (Write a clear, specific goal):
_____
_____
_____
_____
_____
_____
_____

How is this dream relevant to your life?
_____
_____
_____
_____
_____
_____

Achieve by (Date):
___/___/___

Track your progress:

Date	Accomplishments

Trust the process...

Reflect (Lessons Learned):
_____
_____
_____
_____
_____
_____
_____
_____
_____

Encourage yourself:
_____
_____
_____
_____
_____
_____
_____
_____
_____
_____

Date Goal completed:
_____

How will you celebrate?
_____
_____
_____
_____
_____

© Superior Works Publishing 2022

Draw/Plan/Notes:

Date:
____/____/____

Dream/Goal (Write a clear, specific goal):
_____
_____
_____
_____
_____
_____
_____

How is this dream relevant to your life?
_____
_____
_____
_____
_____
_____

Achieve by (Date):
____/____/____

Track your progress:

Date	Accomplishments

Trust the process...

Reflect (Lessons Learned):
_____
_____
_____
_____
_____
_____
_____
_____

Encourage yourself:
_____
_____
_____
_____
_____
_____
_____
_____
_____

Date Goal completed:
_____

How will you celebrate?
_____
_____
_____
_____
_____

© Superior Works Publishing 2022

Draw/Plan/Notes:

Date:
___/___/___

Dream/Goal (Write a clear, specific goal):
_____
_____
_____
_____
_____
_____
_____

How is this dream relevant to your life?
_____
_____
_____
_____
_____
_____

Achieve by (Date):
___/___/_____

Track your progress:

Date	Accomplishments

Trust the process...

Reflect (Lessons Learned):
_____
_____
_____
_____
_____
_____
_____
_____
_____

Encourage yourself:
_____
_____
_____
_____
_____
_____
_____
_____
_____

Date Goal completed:
_____

How will you celebrate?
_____
_____
_____
_____
_____

© Superior Works Publishing 2022

Draw/Plan/Notes:

Date: ____/____/____

Dream/Goal (Write a clear, specific goal):
_____
_____
_____
_____
_____
_____
_____

How is this dream relevant to your life?
_____
_____
_____
_____
_____

Achieve by (Date): ____/____/_____

Track your progress:

Date	Accomplishments

Trust the process…

Reflect (Lessons Learned):
_____
_____
_____
_____
_____
_____
_____
_____
_____

Encourage yourself:
_____
_____
_____
_____
_____
_____
_____
_____
_____
_____

Date Goal completed:
_____

How will you celebrate?
_____
_____
_____
_____
_____

© Superior Works Publishing 2022

Draw/Plan/Notes:

Date:
____/____/____

Dream/Goal (Write a clear, specific goal):
_____
_____
_____
_____
_____
_____
_____

How is this dream relevant to your life?
_____
_____
_____
_____
_____
_____

Achieve by (Date):
____/____/____

Track your progress:

Date	Accomplishments

Trust the process…

Reflect (Lessons Learned):
_____
_____
_____
_____
_____
_____
_____

Encourage yourself:
_____
_____
_____
_____
_____
_____
_____
_____

Date Goal completed:
_____

How will you celebrate?
_____
_____
_____
_____
_____

© Superior Works Publishing 2022

Draw/Plan/Notes:

Date:
____/____/____

Dream/Goal (Write a clear, specific goal):
_____
_____
_____
_____
_____
_____
_____

How is this dream relevant to your life?
_____
_____
_____
_____
_____
_____

Achieve by (Date):
____/____/____

Track your progress:

Date	Accomplishments

Trust the process…

Reflect (Lessons Learned):
_____
_____
_____
_____
_____
_____
_____

Encourage yourself:
_____
_____
_____
_____
_____
_____
_____
_____
_____

Date Goal completed:
_____

How will you celebrate?
_____
_____
_____
_____

© Superior Works Publishing 2022

Draw/Plan/Notes:

Date:
____/____/____

Dream/Goal (Write a clear, specific goal):
_____
_____
_____
_____
_____
_____
_____

How is this dream relevant to your life?
_____
_____
_____
_____
_____
_____

Achieve by (Date):
____/____/____

Track your progress:

Date	Accomplishments

Trust the process…

Reflect (Lessons Learned):
_____
_____
_____
_____
_____
_____
_____
_____

Encourage yourself:
_____
_____
_____
_____
_____
_____
_____
_____

Date Goal completed:
_____

How will you celebrate?
_____
_____
_____
_____
_____

© Superior Works Publishing 2022

Draw/Plan/Notes:

Date:
___/___/___

Dream/Goal (Write a clear, specific goal):
_____
_____
_____
_____
_____
_____
_____

How is this dream relevant to your life?
_____
_____
_____
_____
_____
_____

Achieve by (Date):
___/___/___

Track your progress:

Date	Accomplishments

Trust the process…

Reflect (Lessons Learned):
_____
_____
_____
_____
_____
_____
_____
_____
_____

Encourage yourself:
_____
_____
_____
_____
_____
_____
_____
_____
_____
_____

Date Goal completed:
_____

How will you celebrate?
_____
_____
_____
_____
_____

© Superior Works Publishing 2022

Draw/Plan/Notes:

Date: ____/____/____

Dream/Goal (Write a clear, specific goal):
_____
_____
_____
_____
_____
_____
_____

How is this dream relevant to your life?
_____
_____
_____
_____
_____
_____

Achieve by (Date): ____/____/____

Track your progress:

Date	Accomplishments

Trust the process...

Reflect (Lessons Learned):
_____
_____
_____
_____
_____
_____
_____
_____

Encourage yourself:
_____
_____
_____
_____
_____
_____
_____
_____
_____

Date Goal completed:
_____

How will you celebrate?
_____
_____
_____
_____

© Superior Works Publishing 2022

Draw/Plan/Notes:

Date:
____/____/____

How is this dream relevant to your life?
_____
_____
_____
_____
_____
_____

Dream/Goal (Write a clear, specific goal):
_____
_____
_____
_____
_____
_____
_____
_____

Achieve by (Date):
____/____/_____

Track your progress:

Date	Accomplishments

Trust the process…

Reflect (Lessons Learned):
_____
_____
_____
_____
_____
_____
_____
_____
_____

Encourage yourself:
_____
_____
_____
_____
_____
_____
_____
_____
_____
_____

Date Goal completed:
_____

How will you celebrate?
_____
_____
_____
_____
_____

© Superior Works Publishing 2022

Draw/Plan/Notes:

Date:
____/____/____

Dream/Goal (Write a clear, specific goal):
_____
_____
_____
_____
_____
_____
_____

How is this dream relevant to your life?
_____
_____
_____
_____
_____
_____

Achieve by (Date):
____/____/____

Track your progress:

Date	Accomplishments

Trust the process…

Reflect (Lessons Learned):
_____
_____
_____
_____
_____
_____
_____
_____

Encourage yourself:
_____
_____
_____
_____
_____
_____
_____
_____
_____

Date Goal completed:
_____

How will you celebrate?
_____
_____
_____
_____
_____

© Superior Works Publishing 2022

Draw/Plan/Notes:

Date:
____/____/____

Dream/Goal (Write a clear, specific goal):
_____
_____
_____
_____
_____
_____
_____

How is this dream relevant to your life?
_____
_____
_____
_____
_____
_____

Achieve by (Date):
____/____/_____

Track your progress:

Date	Accomplishments

Trust the process…

Reflect (Lessons Learned):
_____
_____
_____
_____
_____
_____
_____
_____
_____
_____

Encourage yourself:
_____
_____
_____
_____
_____
_____
_____
_____
_____
_____
_____

Date Goal completed:
_____

How will you celebrate?
_____
_____
_____
_____
_____

© Superior Works Publishing 2022

Draw/Plan/Notes:

Date:
____/____/____

Dream/Goal (Write a clear, specific goal):
_____
_____
_____
_____
_____
_____
_____
_____

How is this dream relevant to your life?
_____
_____
_____
_____
_____
_____

Achieve by (Date):
____/____/_____

Track your progress:

Date	Accomplishments

Trust the process…

Reflect (Lessons Learned):
_____
_____
_____
_____
_____
_____
_____
_____

Encourage yourself:
_____
_____
_____
_____
_____
_____
_____
_____

Date Goal completed:
_____

How will you celebrate?
_____
_____
_____
_____
_____

© Superior Works Publishing 2022

Draw/Plan/Notes:

Date: ___/___/___

Dream/Goal (Write a clear, specific goal):
_____
_____
_____
_____
_____
_____
_____

How is this dream relevant to your life?
_____
_____
_____
_____
_____

Achieve by (Date): ___/___/_____

Track your progress:

Date	Accomplishments

Trust the process…

Reflect (Lessons Learned):
_____
_____
_____
_____
_____
_____
_____

Encourage yourself:
_____
_____
_____
_____
_____
_____
_____
_____

Date Goal completed:
_____

How will you celebrate?
_____
_____
_____
_____

© Superior Works Publishing 2022

Draw/Plan/Notes:

Date:
____/____/____

Dream/Goal (Write a clear, specific goal):
_____
_____
_____
_____
_____
_____
_____

How is this dream relevant to your life?
_____
_____
_____
_____
_____
_____

Achieve by (Date):
____/____/_____

Track your progress:

Date	Accomplishments

Trust the process…

Reflect (Lessons Learned):
_____
_____
_____
_____
_____
_____
_____
_____
_____

Encourage yourself:
_____
_____
_____
_____
_____
_____
_____
_____
_____
_____
_____

Date Goal completed:
_____

How will you celebrate?
_____
_____
_____
_____
_____

© Superior Works Publishing 2022

Draw/Plan/Notes:

Date: ____/____/____

Dream/Goal (Write a clear, specific goal):
_____
_____
_____
_____
_____
_____
_____

How is this dream relevant to your life?
_____
_____
_____
_____
_____
_____

Achieve by (Date): ____/____/_____

Track your progress:

Date	Accomplishments

Trust the process…

Reflect (Lessons Learned):
_____
_____
_____
_____
_____
_____
_____
_____
_____

Encourage yourself:
_____
_____
_____
_____
_____
_____
_____
_____
_____

Date Goal completed:
_____

How will you celebrate?
_____
_____
_____
_____
_____

© Superior Works Publishing 2022

Draw/Plan/Notes:

Date:
____/____/____

Dream/Goal (Write a clear, specific goal):
_____
_____
_____
_____
_____
_____
_____

How is this dream relevant to your life?
_____
_____
_____
_____
_____
_____

Achieve by (Date):
____/____/_____

Track your progress:

Date	Accomplishments

Trust the process…

Reflect (Lessons Learned):
_____
_____
_____
_____
_____
_____
_____
_____

Encourage yourself:
_____
_____
_____
_____
_____
_____
_____
_____
_____

Date Goal completed:
_____

How will you celebrate?
_____
_____
_____
_____
_____

© Superior Works Publishing 2022

Draw/Plan/Notes:

Date: ____/____/____

Dream/Goal (Write a clear, specific goal):
_____
_____
_____
_____
_____
_____
_____
_____

How is this dream relevant to your life?
_____
_____
_____
_____
_____

Achieve by (Date): ____/____/_____

Track your progress:

Date	Accomplishments

Trust the process…

Reflect (Lessons Learned):
_____
_____
_____
_____
_____
_____
_____
_____
_____

Encourage yourself:
_____
_____
_____
_____
_____
_____
_____
_____
_____
_____

Date Goal completed:
_____

How will you celebrate?
_____
_____
_____
_____
_____

© Superior Works Publishing 2022

Draw/Plan/Notes:

Date:
____/____/____

Dream/Goal (Write a clear, specific goal):
_____
_____
_____
_____
_____
_____
_____

How is this dream relevant to your life?
_____
_____
_____
_____
_____
_____

Achieve by (Date):
____/____/____

Track your progress:

Date	Accomplishments

Trust the process…

Reflect (Lessons Learned):
_____
_____
_____
_____
_____
_____
_____
_____
_____

Encourage yourself:
_____
_____
_____
_____
_____
_____
_____
_____
_____
_____

Date Goal completed:
_____

How will you celebrate?
_____
_____
_____
_____
_____

Draw/Plan/Notes:

Date:
____/____/____

How is this dream relevant to your life?
_____
_____
_____
_____
_____

Dream/Goal (Write a clear, specific goal):
_____
_____
_____
_____
_____
_____
_____

Achieve by (Date):
____/____/_____

Track your progress:

Date	Accomplishments

Trust the process…

Reflect (Lessons Learned):
_____
_____
_____
_____
_____
_____
_____
_____
_____

Encourage yourself:
_____
_____
_____
_____
_____
_____
_____
_____
_____

Date Goal completed:
_____

How will you celebrate?
_____
_____
_____
_____
_____

© Superior Works Publishing 2022

Draw/Plan/Notes:

Date:
___/___/___

Dream/Goal (Write a clear, specific goal):
_____
_____
_____
_____
_____
_____
_____

How is this dream relevant to your life?
_____
_____
_____
_____
_____
_____

Achieve by (Date):
___/___/___

Track your progress:

Date	Accomplishments

Trust the process...

Reflect (Lessons Learned):
_____
_____
_____
_____
_____
_____
_____
_____

Encourage yourself:
_____
_____
_____
_____
_____
_____
_____
_____
_____

Date Goal completed:
_____

How will you celebrate?
_____
_____
_____
_____
_____

© Superior Works Publishing 2022

Draw/Plan/Notes:

Date: ___/___/___

Dream/Goal (Write a clear, specific goal):
_____
_____
_____
_____
_____
_____
_____

How is this dream relevant to your life?
_____
_____
_____
_____
_____

Achieve by (Date): ___/___/_____

Track your progress:

Date	Accomplishments

Trust the process…

Reflect (Lessons Learned):
_____
_____
_____
_____
_____
_____
_____
_____

Encourage yourself:
_____
_____
_____
_____
_____
_____
_____
_____
_____

Date Goal completed:
_____

How will you celebrate?
_____
_____
_____
_____
_____

© Superior Works Publishing 2022

Draw/Plan/Notes:

Date:
____/____/____

Dream/Goal (Write a clear, specific goal):
_____
_____
_____
_____
_____
_____
_____
_____

How is this dream relevant to your life?
_____
_____
_____
_____
_____

Achieve by (Date):
____/____/_____

Track your progress:

Date	Accomplishments

Trust the process…

Reflect (Lessons Learned):
_____
_____
_____
_____
_____
_____
_____
_____

Encourage yourself:
_____
_____
_____
_____
_____
_____
_____
_____
_____
_____

Date Goal completed:
_____

How will you celebrate?
_____
_____
_____
_____
_____

© Superior Works Publishing 2022

Draw/Plan/Notes:

Date: ___/___/___

Dream/Goal (Write a clear, specific goal):
_____
_____
_____
_____
_____
_____
_____
_____

How is this dream relevant to your life?
_____
_____
_____
_____
_____
_____

Achieve by (Date): ___/___/_____

Track your progress:

Date	Accomplishments

Trust the process...

Reflect (Lessons Learned):
_____
_____
_____
_____
_____
_____
_____
_____
_____

Encourage yourself:
_____
_____
_____
_____
_____
_____
_____
_____
_____

Date Goal completed:
_____

How will you celebrate?
_____
_____
_____
_____
_____

© Superior Works Publishing 2022

Draw/Plan/Notes:

Date: ___/___/___

Dream/Goal (Write a clear, specific goal):
_____
_____
_____
_____
_____
_____
_____
_____

How is this dream relevant to your life?
_____
_____
_____
_____
_____
_____

Achieve by (Date): ___/___/_____

Track your progress:

Date	Accomplishments

Trust the process…

Reflect (Lessons Learned):
_____
_____
_____
_____
_____
_____
_____
_____
_____

Encourage yourself:
_____
_____
_____
_____
_____
_____
_____
_____
_____
_____

Date Goal completed:
_____

How will you celebrate?
_____
_____
_____
_____
_____

© Superior Works Publishing 2022

Draw/Plan/Notes:

Date: ___/___/___

Dream/Goal (Write a clear, specific goal):
_____
_____
_____
_____
_____
_____
_____

How is this dream relevant to your life?
_____
_____
_____
_____
_____

Achieve by (Date): ___/___/_____

Track your progress:

Date	Accomplishments

Trust the process...

Reflect (Lessons Learned):
_____
_____
_____
_____
_____
_____
_____
_____
_____

Encourage yourself:
_____
_____
_____
_____
_____
_____
_____
_____
_____

Date Goal completed:
_____

How will you celebrate?
_____
_____
_____
_____
_____

© Superior Works Publishing 2022

Draw/Plan/Notes:

Date:
____/____/____

Dream/Goal (Write a clear, specific goal):
_____
_____
_____
_____
_____
_____
_____

How is this dream relevant to your life?
_____
_____
_____
_____
_____

Achieve by (Date):
____/____/_____

Track your progress:

Date	Accomplishments

Trust the process…

Reflect (Lessons Learned):
_____
_____
_____
_____
_____
_____
_____
_____
_____

Encourage yourself:
_____
_____
_____
_____
_____
_____
_____
_____
_____
_____

Date Goal completed:
_____

How will you celebrate?
_____
_____
_____
_____
_____

© Superior Works Publishing 2022

Draw/Plan/Notes:

Date:
____/____/____

How is this dream relevant to your life?
_____
_____
_____
_____
_____
_____

Dream/Goal (Write a clear, specific goal):
_____
_____
_____
_____
_____
_____
_____

Achieve by (Date):
____/____/_____

Track your progress:

Date	Accomplishments

Trust the process...

Reflect (Lessons Learned):
_____
_____
_____
_____
_____
_____
_____
_____

Encourage yourself:
_____
_____
_____
_____
_____
_____
_____
_____
_____

Date Goal completed:
_____

How will you celebrate?
_____
_____
_____
_____
_____

© Superior Works Publishing 2022

Draw/Plan/Notes:

Date: ___/___/___

Dream/Goal (Write a clear, specific goal):
_____
_____
_____
_____
_____
_____
_____
_____

How is this dream relevant to your life?
_____
_____
_____
_____
_____

Achieve by (Date): ___/___/_____

Track your progress:

Date	Accomplishments

Trust the process…

Reflect (Lessons Learned):
_____
_____
_____
_____
_____
_____
_____
_____

Encourage yourself:
_____
_____
_____
_____
_____
_____
_____
_____
_____

Date Goal completed:
_____

How will you celebrate?
_____
_____
_____
_____
_____

© Superior Works Publishing 2022

Draw/Plan/Notes:

Date:	Dream/Goal (Write a clear, specific goal):
____/____/____	

How is this dream relevant to your life?

_____
_____
_____
_____
_____

Achieve by (Date):
____/____/_____

Track your progress:

Date	Accomplishments

Trust the process…

Reflect (Lessons Learned):

_____
_____
_____
_____
_____
_____
_____
_____

Encourage yourself:

_____
_____
_____
_____
_____
_____
_____
_____
_____

Date Goal completed:
_____

How will you celebrate?

_____
_____
_____
_____
_____

© Superior Works Publishing 2022

Draw/Plan/Notes:

© Superior Works Publishing 2022

Date:
____/____/____

Dream/Goal (Write a clear, specific goal):
_____
_____
_____
_____
_____
_____
_____

How is this dream relevant to your life?
_____
_____
_____
_____
_____
_____

Achieve by (Date):
____/____/_____

Track your progress:

Date	Accomplishments

Trust the process…

Reflect (Lessons Learned):
_____
_____
_____
_____
_____
_____
_____
_____
_____

Encourage yourself:
_____
_____
_____
_____
_____
_____
_____
_____
_____
_____

Date Goal completed:
_____

How will you celebrate?
_____
_____
_____
_____
_____

© Superior Works Publishing 2022

Draw/Plan/Notes:

© Superior Works Publishing 2022

Date:
____/____/____

How is this dream relevant to your life?
_____
_____
_____
_____
_____
_____

Dream/Goal (Write a clear, specific goal):
_____
_____
_____
_____
_____
_____
_____
_____

Achieve by (Date):
____/____/_____

Track your progress:

Date	Accomplishments

Trust the process...

Reflect (Lessons Learned):
_____
_____
_____
_____
_____
_____
_____
_____
_____

Encourage yourself:
_____
_____
_____
_____
_____
_____
_____
_____
_____
_____

Date Goal completed:
_____

How will you celebrate?
_____
_____
_____
_____
_____

© Superior Works Publishing 2022

Draw/Plan/Notes:

Date:
____/____/____

Dream/Goal (Write a clear, specific goal):
_____
_____
_____
_____
_____
_____

How is this dream relevant to your life?
_____
_____
_____
_____
_____

Achieve by (Date):
____/____/_____

Track your progress:

Date	Accomplishments

Trust the process...

Reflect (Lessons Learned):
_____
_____
_____
_____
_____
_____
_____
_____

Encourage yourself:
_____
_____
_____
_____
_____
_____
_____
_____
_____
_____

Date Goal completed:
_____

How will you celebrate?
_____
_____
_____
_____
_____

© Superior Works Publishing 2022

Draw/Plan/Notes:

Date:
____/____/____

Dream/Goal (Write a clear, specific goal):
_____
_____
_____
_____
_____
_____
_____

How is this dream relevant to your life?
_____
_____
_____
_____
_____

Achieve by (Date):
____/____/_____

Track your progress:

Date	Accomplishments

Trust the process…

Reflect (Lessons Learned):
_____
_____
_____
_____
_____
_____
_____
_____

Encourage yourself:
_____
_____
_____
_____
_____
_____
_____
_____

Date Goal completed:
_____

How will you celebrate?
_____
_____
_____
_____
_____

© Superior Works Publishing 2022

Draw/Plan/Notes:

Date:
___/___/___

Dream/Goal (Write a clear, specific goal):
_____
_____
_____
_____
_____
_____
_____

How is this dream relevant to your life?
_____
_____
_____
_____
_____

Achieve by (Date):
___/___/_____

Track your progress:

Date	Accomplishments

Trust the process…

Reflect (Lessons Learned):
_____
_____
_____
_____
_____
_____
_____
_____
_____

Encourage yourself:
_____
_____
_____
_____
_____
_____
_____
_____
_____
_____

Date Goal completed:
_____

How will you celebrate?
_____
_____
_____
_____
_____

© Superior Works Publishing 2022

Draw/Plan/Notes:

Date: ___/___/___

Dream/Goal (Write a clear, specific goal):
_____
_____
_____
_____
_____
_____
_____

How is this dream relevant to your life?
_____
_____
_____
_____
_____

Achieve by (Date): ___/___/_____

Track your progress:

Date	Accomplishments

Trust the process…

Reflect (Lessons Learned):
_____
_____
_____
_____
_____
_____
_____
_____

Encourage yourself:
_____
_____
_____
_____
_____
_____
_____
_____
_____

Date Goal completed:
_____

How will you celebrate?
_____
_____
_____
_____
_____

© Superior Works Publishing 2022

Draw/Plan/Notes:

Date: ___/___/___

Dream/Goal (Write a clear, specific goal):
_____
_____
_____
_____
_____
_____
_____

How is this dream relevant to your life?
_____
_____
_____
_____
_____
_____

Achieve by (Date): ___/___/_____

Track your progress:

Date	Accomplishments

Trust the process...

Reflect (Lessons Learned):
_____
_____
_____
_____
_____
_____
_____
_____
_____

Encourage yourself:
_____
_____
_____
_____
_____
_____
_____
_____
_____
_____

Date Goal completed:
_____

How will you celebrate?
_____
_____
_____
_____
_____
_____

© Superior Works Publishing 2022

Draw/Plan/Notes:

Date:
____/____/____

Dream/Goal (Write a clear, specific goal):
_____
_____
_____
_____
_____
_____
_____

How is this dream relevant to your life?
_____
_____
_____
_____
_____
_____

Achieve by (Date):
____/____/_____

Track your progress:

Date	Accomplishments

Trust the process...

Reflect (Lessons Learned):
_____
_____
_____
_____
_____
_____
_____
_____
_____
_____

Encourage yourself:
_____
_____
_____
_____
_____
_____
_____
_____
_____
_____

Date Goal completed:
_____

How will you celebrate?
_____
_____
_____
_____
_____

© Superior Works Publishing 2022

Draw/Plan/Notes:

Date:
____/____/____

Dream/Goal (Write a clear, specific goal):
_____
_____
_____
_____
_____
_____
_____

How is this dream relevant to your life?
_____
_____
_____
_____
_____

Achieve by (Date):
____/____/_____

Track your progress:

Date	Accomplishments

Trust the process...

Reflect (Lessons Learned):
_____
_____
_____
_____
_____
_____
_____
_____

Encourage yourself:
_____
_____
_____
_____
_____
_____
_____
_____
_____

Date Goal completed:
_____

How will you celebrate?
_____
_____
_____
_____
_____

Draw/Plan/Notes:

© Superior Works Publishing 2022

Date:
____/____/____

How is this dream relevant to your life?
_____
_____
_____
_____
_____

Dream/Goal (Write a clear, specific goal):
_____
_____
_____
_____
_____
_____
_____
_____

Achieve by (Date):
____/____/_____

Track your progress:

Date	Accomplishments

Trust the process…

Reflect (Lessons Learned):
_____
_____
_____
_____
_____
_____
_____
_____
_____

Encourage yourself:
_____
_____
_____
_____
_____
_____
_____
_____
_____
_____

Date Goal completed:
_____

How will you celebrate?
_____
_____
_____
_____
_____

© Superior Works Publishing 2022

Draw/Plan/Notes:

Date:
____/____/____

Dream/Goal (Write a clear, specific goal):
_____
_____
_____
_____
_____
_____
_____

How is this dream relevant to your life?
_____
_____
_____
_____
_____
_____

Achieve by (Date):
____/____/_____

Track your progress:

Date	Accomplishments

Trust the process...

Reflect (Lessons Learned):
_____
_____
_____
_____
_____
_____
_____
_____
_____

Encourage yourself:
_____
_____
_____
_____
_____
_____
_____
_____
_____

Date Goal completed:
_____

How will you celebrate?
_____
_____
_____
_____
_____

© Superior Works Publishing 2022

Draw/Plan/Notes:

Date:
___/___/___

How is this dream relevant to your life?
_____
_____
_____
_____
_____
_____

Dream/Goal (Write a clear, specific goal):
_____
_____
_____
_____
_____
_____
_____
_____

Achieve by (Date):
___/___/___

Track your progress:

Date	Accomplishments

Trust the process…

Reflect (Lessons Learned):
_____
_____
_____
_____
_____
_____
_____
_____
_____

Encourage yourself:
_____
_____
_____
_____
_____
_____
_____
_____
_____

Date Goal completed:
_____

How will you celebrate?
_____
_____
_____
_____
_____

© Superior Works Publishing 2022

Draw/Plan/Notes:

Date: ___/___/___

Dream/Goal (Write a clear, specific goal):
_____
_____
_____
_____
_____
_____
_____

How is this dream relevant to your life?
_____
_____
_____
_____
_____

Achieve by (Date): ___/___/_____

Track your progress:

Date	Accomplishments

Trust the process…

Reflect (Lessons Learned):
_____
_____
_____
_____
_____
_____
_____
_____
_____

Encourage yourself:
_____
_____
_____
_____
_____
_____
_____
_____
_____

Date Goal completed:
_____

How will you celebrate?
_____
_____
_____
_____
_____

© Superior Works Publishing 2022

Draw/Plan/Notes:

Date:
____/____/____

How is this dream relevant to your life?
_____
_____
_____
_____
_____

Dream/Goal (Write a clear, specific goal):
_____
_____
_____
_____
_____
_____
_____

Achieve by (Date):
____/____/_____

Track your progress:

Date	Accomplishments

Trust the process...

Reflect (Lessons Learned):
_____
_____
_____
_____
_____
_____
_____
_____
_____

Encourage yourself:
_____
_____
_____
_____
_____
_____
_____
_____
_____

Date Goal completed:
_____

How will you celebrate?
_____
_____
_____
_____
_____

© Superior Works Publishing 2022

Draw/Plan/Notes:

Date:
____/____/____

Dream/Goal (Write a clear, specific goal):
_____
_____
_____
_____
_____
_____
_____
_____

How is this dream relevant to your life?
_____
_____
_____
_____
_____

Achieve by (Date):
____/____/____

Track your progress:

Date	Accomplishments

Trust the process…

Reflect (Lessons Learned):
_____
_____
_____
_____
_____
_____
_____
_____

Encourage yourself:
_____
_____
_____
_____
_____
_____
_____
_____
_____

Date Goal completed:
_____

How will you celebrate?
_____
_____
_____
_____
_____

© Superior Works Publishing 2022

Draw/Plan/Notes:

Date:
____/____/____

Dream/Goal (Write a clear, specific goal):
_____
_____
_____
_____
_____
_____
_____

How is this dream relevant to your life?
_____
_____
_____
_____
_____

Achieve by (Date):
____/____/____

Track your progress:

Date	Accomplishments

Trust the process…

Reflect (Lessons Learned):
_____
_____
_____
_____
_____
_____
_____
_____
_____

Encourage yourself:
_____
_____
_____
_____
_____
_____
_____
_____
_____
_____

Date Goal completed:
_____

How will you celebrate?
_____
_____
_____
_____
_____

© Superior Works Publishing 2022

Draw/Plan/Notes:

Date: ____/____/____

Dream/Goal (Write a clear, specific goal):
_____
_____
_____
_____
_____
_____
_____

How is this dream relevant to your life?
_____
_____
_____
_____
_____

Achieve by (Date): ____/____/____

Track your progress:

Date	Accomplishments

Trust the process...

Reflect (Lessons Learned):
_____
_____
_____
_____
_____
_____
_____
_____

Encourage yourself:
_____
_____
_____
_____
_____
_____
_____
_____
_____
_____

Date Goal completed:
_____

How will you celebrate?
_____
_____
_____
_____
_____

© Superior Works Publishing 2022

Draw/Plan/Notes:

Date: ___/___/___	Dream/Goal (Write a clear, specific goal):

How is this dream relevant to your life?
_____
_____
_____
_____
_____

Achieve by (Date): ___/___/_____

Track your progress:

Date	Accomplishments

Trust the process…

Reflect (Lessons Learned):
_____
_____
_____
_____
_____
_____
_____
_____

Encourage yourself:
_____
_____
_____
_____
_____
_____
_____
_____
_____

Date Goal completed:
_____

How will you celebrate?
_____
_____
_____
_____
_____

© Superior Works Publishing 2022

Draw/Plan/Notes:

© Superior Works Publishing 2022

Date:
___/___/___

Dream/Goal (Write a clear, specific goal):
_____
_____
_____
_____
_____
_____
_____

How is this dream relevant to your life?
_____
_____
_____
_____
_____
_____

Achieve by (Date):
___/___/___

Track your progress:

Date	Accomplishments

Trust the process…

Reflect (Lessons Learned):
_____
_____
_____
_____
_____
_____
_____
_____
_____

Encourage yourself:
_____
_____
_____
_____
_____
_____
_____
_____
_____

Date Goal completed:
_____

How will you celebrate?
_____
_____
_____
_____
_____

© Superior Works Publishing 2022

Draw/Plan/Notes:

Date:
____/____/____

Dream/Goal (Write a clear, specific goal):
_____
_____
_____
_____
_____
_____
_____

How is this dream relevant to your life?
_____
_____
_____
_____

Achieve by (Date):
____/____/____

Track your progress:

Date	Accomplishments

Trust the process...

Reflect (Lessons Learned):
_____
_____
_____
_____
_____
_____
_____

Encourage yourself:
_____
_____
_____
_____
_____
_____
_____
_____

Date Goal completed:
_____

How will you celebrate?
_____
_____
_____
_____

© Superior Works Publishing 2022

Draw/Plan/Notes:

Date:
____/____/____

Dream/Goal (Write a clear, specific goal):
_____
_____
_____
_____
_____
_____
_____

How is this dream relevant to your life?
_____
_____
_____
_____
_____

Achieve by (Date):
____/____/_____

Track your progress:

Date	Accomplishments

Trust the process...

Reflect (Lessons Learned):
_____
_____
_____
_____
_____
_____
_____
_____
_____

Encourage yourself:
_____
_____
_____
_____
_____
_____
_____
_____
_____
_____

Date Goal completed:
_____

How will you celebrate?
_____
_____
_____
_____
_____

© Superior Works Publishing 2022

Draw/Plan/Notes:

© Superior Works Publishing 2022

Date:
____/____/____

Dream/Goal (Write a clear, specific goal):
_____
_____
_____
_____
_____
_____
_____

How is this dream relevant to your life?
_____
_____
_____
_____
_____

Achieve by (Date):
____/____/_____

Track your progress:

Date	Accomplishments

Trust the process...

Reflect (Lessons Learned):
_____
_____
_____
_____
_____
_____
_____
_____
_____

Encourage yourself:
_____
_____
_____
_____
_____
_____
_____
_____
_____
_____

Date Goal completed:
_____

How will you celebrate?
_____
_____
_____
_____
_____

© Superior Works Publishing 2022

Draw/Plan/Notes:

Date:
___/___/___

How is this dream relevant to your life?
_____
_____
_____
_____
_____

Dream/Goal (Write a clear, specific goal):
_____
_____
_____
_____
_____
_____
_____

Achieve by (Date):
___/___/_____

Track your progress:

Date	Accomplishments

Trust the process…

Reflect (Lessons Learned):
_____
_____
_____
_____
_____
_____
_____
_____
_____

Encourage yourself:
_____
_____
_____
_____
_____
_____
_____
_____
_____
_____

Date Goal completed:
_____

How will you celebrate?
_____
_____
_____
_____
_____

© Superior Works Publishing 2022

Draw/Plan/Notes:

Date: ___/___/___

Dream/Goal (Write a clear, specific goal):
_____
_____
_____
_____
_____
_____
_____

How is this dream relevant to your life?
_____
_____
_____
_____
_____

Achieve by (Date): ___/___/_____

Track your progress:

Date	Accomplishments

Trust the process…

Reflect (Lessons Learned):
_____
_____
_____
_____
_____
_____
_____
_____

Encourage yourself:
_____
_____
_____
_____
_____
_____
_____
_____
_____

Date Goal completed:
_____

How will you celebrate?
_____
_____
_____
_____
_____

© Superior Works Publishing 2022

Draw/Plan/Notes:

Date:
____/____/____

Dream/Goal (Write a clear, specific goal):
_____
_____
_____
_____
_____
_____
_____

How is this dream relevant to your life?
_____
_____
_____
_____
_____

Achieve by (Date):
____/____/_____

Track your progress:

Date	Accomplishments

Trust the process…

Reflect (Lessons Learned):
_____
_____
_____
_____
_____
_____
_____
_____

Encourage yourself:
_____
_____
_____
_____
_____
_____
_____
_____

Date Goal completed:
_____

How will you celebrate?
_____
_____
_____
_____
_____

© Superior Works Publishing 2022

Draw/Plan/Notes:

Date:
___/___/___

Dream/Goal (Write a clear, specific goal):
_____
_____
_____
_____
_____
_____
_____
_____

How is this dream relevant to your life?
_____
_____
_____
_____
_____

Achieve by (Date):
___/___/_____

Track your progress:

Date	Accomplishments

Trust the process…

Reflect (Lessons Learned):
_____
_____
_____
_____
_____
_____
_____
_____

Encourage yourself:
_____
_____
_____
_____
_____
_____
_____
_____
_____
_____

Date Goal completed:
_____

How will you celebrate?
_____
_____
_____
_____
_____

© Superior Works Publishing 2022

Draw/Plan/Notes:

Date: ___/___/___	Dream/Goal (Write a clear, specific goal):

_____
_____
_____
_____
_____
_____
_____

How is this dream relevant to your life?
_____
_____
_____
_____
_____

Achieve by (Date): ___/___/_____

Track your progress:

Date	Accomplishments

Trust the process…

Reflect (Lessons Learned):
_____
_____
_____
_____
_____
_____
_____
_____
_____

Encourage yourself:
_____
_____
_____
_____
_____
_____
_____
_____
_____

Date Goal completed:
_____

How will you celebrate?
_____
_____
_____
_____
_____

Draw/Plan/Notes:

Date: ____/____/____

Dream/Goal (Write a clear, specific goal):
_____
_____
_____
_____
_____
_____
_____
_____

How is this dream relevant to your life?
_____
_____
_____
_____
_____

Achieve by (Date): ____/____/_____

Track your progress:

Date	Accomplishments

Trust the process...

Reflect (Lessons Learned):
_____
_____
_____
_____
_____
_____
_____
_____
_____

Encourage yourself:
_____
_____
_____
_____
_____
_____
_____
_____
_____
_____

Date Goal completed:
_____

How will you celebrate?
_____
_____
_____
_____
_____

© Superior Works Publishing 2022

Draw/Plan/Notes:

Date: ___/___/___

How is this dream relevant to your life?
_____
_____
_____
_____
_____

Dream/Goal (Write a clear, specific goal):
_____
_____
_____
_____
_____
_____
_____

Achieve by (Date): ___/___/_____

Track your progress:

Date	Accomplishments

Trust the process…

Reflect (Lessons Learned):
_____
_____
_____
_____
_____
_____
_____
_____
_____

Encourage yourself:
_____
_____
_____
_____
_____
_____
_____
_____
_____
_____

Date Goal completed:
_____

How will you celebrate?
_____
_____
_____
_____
_____

© Superior Works Publishing 2022

Draw/Plan/Notes:

© Superior Works Publishing 2022

Date: ___/___/___	Dream/Goal (Write a clear, specific goal):

_____
_____
_____
_____
_____
_____
_____

How is this dream relevant to your life?
_____
_____
_____
_____
_____

Achieve by (Date): ___/___/_____

Track your progress:

Date	Accomplishments

Trust the process…

Reflect (Lessons Learned):
_____
_____
_____
_____
_____
_____
_____
_____
_____

Encourage yourself:
_____
_____
_____
_____
_____
_____
_____
_____
_____
_____
_____

Date Goal completed:
_____

How will you celebrate?
_____
_____
_____
_____
_____

© Superior Works Publishing 2022

Draw/Plan/Notes:

Date: ___/___/___

Dream/Goal (Write a clear, specific goal):
_____
_____
_____
_____
_____
_____
_____

How is this dream relevant to your life?
_____
_____
_____
_____
_____

Achieve by (Date): ___/___/_____

Track your progress:

Date	Accomplishments

Trust the process…

Reflect (Lessons Learned):
_____
_____
_____
_____
_____
_____
_____
_____
_____
_____

Encourage yourself:
_____
_____
_____
_____
_____
_____
_____
_____
_____
_____

Date Goal completed:
_____

How will you celebrate?
_____
_____
_____
_____
_____

© Superior Works Publishing 2022

Draw/Plan/Notes:

Date:
___/___/___

How is this dream relevant to your life?
_____
_____
_____
_____
_____

Dream/Goal (Write a clear, specific goal):
_____
_____
_____
_____
_____
_____
_____
_____

Achieve by (Date):
___/___/_____

Track your progress:

Date	Accomplishments

Trust the process…

Reflect (Lessons Learned):
_____
_____
_____
_____
_____
_____
_____
_____
_____

Encourage yourself:
_____
_____
_____
_____
_____
_____
_____
_____
_____
_____

Date Goal completed:
_____

How will you celebrate?
_____
_____
_____
_____
_____

© Superior Works Publishing 2022

Draw/Plan/Notes:

Date:
____/____/____

Dream/Goal (Write a clear, specific goal):
_____
_____
_____
_____
_____
_____
_____
_____

How is this dream relevant to your life?
_____
_____
_____
_____
_____
_____

Achieve by (Date):
____/____/_____

Track your progress:

Date	Accomplishments

Trust the process…

Reflect (Lessons Learned):
_____
_____
_____
_____
_____
_____
_____
_____

Encourage yourself:
_____
_____
_____
_____
_____
_____
_____
_____
_____

Date Goal completed:
_____

How will you celebrate?
_____
_____
_____
_____
_____

© Superior Works Publishing 2022

Draw/Plan/Notes:

© Superior Works Publishing 2022

Date: ____/____/____

How is this dream relevant to your life?
_____
_____
_____
_____
_____

Dream/Goal (Write a clear, specific goal):
_____
_____
_____
_____
_____
_____
_____
_____

Achieve by (Date): ____/____/_____

Track your progress:

Date	Accomplishments

Trust the process...

Reflect (Lessons Learned):
_____
_____
_____
_____
_____
_____
_____
_____
_____

Encourage yourself:
_____
_____
_____
_____
_____
_____
_____
_____
_____
_____

Date Goal completed:
_____

How will you celebrate?
_____
_____
_____
_____
_____

© Superior Works Publishing 2022

Draw/Plan/Notes:

Date: ___/___/___	Dream/Goal (Write a clear, specific goal):

_____
_____
_____
_____
_____
_____
_____
_____

How is this dream relevant to your life?
_____
_____
_____
_____
_____

Achieve by (Date): ___/___/_____

Track your progress:

Date	Accomplishments

Trust the process…

Reflect (Lessons Learned):
_____
_____
_____
_____
_____
_____
_____
_____
_____

Encourage yourself:
_____
_____
_____
_____
_____
_____
_____
_____
_____
_____

Date Goal completed:
_____

How will you celebrate?
_____
_____
_____
_____
_____

© Superior Works Publishing 2022

Draw/Plan/Notes:

© Superior Works Publishing 2022

Date: ___/___/___

Dream/Goal (Write a clear, specific goal):
_____
_____
_____
_____
_____
_____
_____

How is this dream relevant to your life?
_____
_____
_____
_____
_____

Achieve by (Date): ___/___/_____

Track your progress:

Date	Accomplishments

Trust the process…

Reflect (Lessons Learned):
_____
_____
_____
_____
_____
_____
_____
_____
_____

Encourage yourself:
_____
_____
_____
_____
_____
_____
_____
_____
_____
_____

Date Goal completed:
_____

How will you celebrate?
_____
_____
_____
_____
_____

© Superior Works Publishing 2022

Draw/Plan/Notes:

Date: ___/___/___

Dream/Goal (Write a clear, specific goal):
_____
_____
_____
_____
_____
_____
_____

How is this dream relevant to your life?
_____
_____
_____
_____
_____

Achieve by (Date): ___/___/_____

Track your progress:

Date	Accomplishments

Trust the process…

Reflect (Lessons Learned):
_____
_____
_____
_____
_____
_____
_____
_____
_____

Encourage yourself:
_____
_____
_____
_____
_____
_____
_____
_____
_____

Date Goal completed:
_____

How will you celebrate?
_____
_____
_____
_____

© Superior Works Publishing 2022

Draw/Plan/Notes:

Date:
____/____/____

How is this dream relevant to your life?
_____
_____
_____
_____
_____

Dream/Goal (Write a clear, specific goal):
_____
_____
_____
_____
_____
_____
_____

Achieve by (Date):
____/____/_____

Track your progress:

Date	Accomplishments

Trust the process...

Reflect (Lessons Learned):
_____
_____
_____
_____
_____
_____
_____
_____

Encourage yourself:
_____
_____
_____
_____
_____
_____
_____
_____
_____

Date Goal completed:
_____

How will you celebrate?
_____
_____
_____
_____
_____

© Superior Works Publishing 2022

Draw/Plan/Notes:

Date:
____/____/____

Dream/Goal (Write a clear, specific goal):
_____
_____
_____
_____
_____
_____
_____

How is this dream relevant to your life?
_____
_____
_____
_____
_____

Achieve by (Date):
____/____/_____

Track your progress:

Date	Accomplishments

Trust the process…

Reflect (Lessons Learned):
_____
_____
_____
_____
_____
_____
_____
_____
_____
_____

Encourage yourself:
_____
_____
_____
_____
_____
_____
_____
_____
_____
_____
_____

Date Goal completed:
_____

How will you celebrate?
_____
_____
_____
_____
_____

© Superior Works Publishing 2022

Draw/Plan/Notes:

Date:
___/___/___

How is this dream relevant to your life?
_____
_____
_____
_____
_____

Dream/Goal (Write a clear, specific goal):
_____
_____
_____
_____
_____
_____
_____

Achieve by (Date):
___/___/_____

Track your progress:

Date	Accomplishments

Trust the process...

Reflect (Lessons Learned):
_____
_____
_____
_____
_____
_____
_____
_____
_____

Encourage yourself:
_____
_____
_____
_____
_____
_____
_____
_____
_____
_____

Date Goal completed:
_____

How will you celebrate?
_____
_____
_____
_____
_____

© Superior Works Publishing 2022

Draw/Plan/Notes:

Date: ___/___/___

Dream/Goal (Write a clear, specific goal):
_____
_____
_____
_____
_____
_____
_____

How is this dream relevant to your life?
_____
_____
_____
_____
_____
_____

Achieve by (Date): ___/___/_____

Track your progress:

Date	Accomplishments

Trust the process...

Reflect (Lessons Learned):
_____
_____
_____
_____
_____
_____
_____
_____
_____

Encourage yourself:
_____
_____
_____
_____
_____
_____
_____
_____
_____

Date Goal completed:
_____

How will you celebrate?
_____
_____
_____
_____

© Superior Works Publishing 2022

Draw/Plan/Notes:

Date: ___/___/___

Dream/Goal (Write a clear, specific goal):
_____
_____
_____
_____
_____
_____
_____

How is this dream relevant to your life?
_____
_____
_____
_____
_____

Achieve by (Date): ___/___/_____

Track your progress:

Date	Accomplishments

Trust the process...

Reflect (Lessons Learned):
_____
_____
_____
_____
_____
_____
_____
_____
_____

Encourage yourself:
_____
_____
_____
_____
_____
_____
_____
_____
_____
_____

Date Goal completed:
_____

How will you celebrate?
_____
_____
_____
_____
_____

© Superior Works Publishing 2022

Draw/Plan/Notes:

Date:
___/___/___

Dream/Goal (Write a clear, specific goal):
_____
_____
_____
_____
_____
_____
_____
_____

How is this dream relevant to your life?
_____
_____
_____
_____
_____

Achieve by (Date):
___/___/_____

Track your progress:

Date	Accomplishments

Trust the process…

Reflect (Lessons Learned):
_____
_____
_____
_____
_____
_____
_____
_____

Encourage yourself:
_____
_____
_____
_____
_____
_____
_____
_____
_____
_____

Date Goal completed:
_____

How will you celebrate?
_____
_____
_____
_____
_____

© Superior Works Publishing 2022

Draw/Plan/Notes:

Date:
___/___/___

How is this dream relevant to your life?
_____
_____
_____
_____
_____

Dream/Goal (Write a clear, specific goal):
_____
_____
_____
_____
_____
_____
_____
_____

Achieve by (Date):
___/___/_____

Track your progress:

Date	Accomplishments

Trust the process...

Reflect (Lessons Learned):
_____
_____
_____
_____
_____
_____
_____
_____
_____

Encourage yourself:
_____
_____
_____
_____
_____
_____
_____
_____
_____
_____

Date Goal completed:
_____

How will you celebrate?
_____
_____
_____
_____
_____

© Superior Works Publishing 2022

Draw/Plan/Notes:

Date:
___/___/___

Dream/Goal (Write a clear, specific goal):
_____
_____
_____
_____
_____
_____
_____

How is this dream relevant to your life?
_____
_____
_____
_____
_____

Achieve by (Date):
___/___/___

Track your progress:

Date	Accomplishments

Trust the process…

Reflect (Lessons Learned):
_____
_____
_____
_____
_____
_____
_____
_____

Encourage yourself:
_____
_____
_____
_____
_____
_____
_____
_____
_____
_____

Date Goal completed:
_____

How will you celebrate?
_____
_____
_____
_____
_____

© Superior Works Publishing 2022

Draw/Plan/Notes:

Date:
____/____/____

Dream/Goal (Write a clear, specific goal):
_____
_____
_____
_____
_____
_____
_____

How is this dream relevant to your life?
_____
_____
_____
_____
_____

Achieve by (Date):
____/____/_____

Track your progress:

Date	Accomplishments

Trust the process…

Reflect (Lessons Learned):
_____
_____
_____
_____
_____
_____
_____
_____
_____

Encourage yourself:
_____
_____
_____
_____
_____
_____
_____
_____
_____
_____
_____

Date Goal completed:
_____

How will you celebrate?
_____
_____
_____
_____
_____

© Superior Works Publishing 2022

Draw/Plan/Notes:

Date: ___/___/___	Dream/Goal (Write a clear, specific goal):

_____
_____
_____
_____
_____
_____
_____

How is this dream relevant to your life?
_____
_____
_____
_____
_____

Achieve by (Date): ___/___/_____

Track your progress:

Date	Accomplishments

Trust the process...

Reflect (Lessons Learned):
_____
_____
_____
_____
_____
_____
_____
_____

Encourage yourself:
_____
_____
_____
_____
_____
_____
_____
_____
_____

Date Goal completed:
_____

How will you celebrate?
_____
_____
_____
_____

© Superior Works Publishing 2022

Draw/Plan/Notes:

Date:
___/___/___

Dream/Goal (Write a clear, specific goal):
_____
_____
_____
_____
_____
_____
_____
_____

How is this dream relevant to your life?
_____
_____
_____
_____
_____

Achieve by (Date):
___/___/_____

Track your progress:

Date	Accomplishments

Trust the process...

Reflect (Lessons Learned):
_____
_____
_____
_____
_____
_____
_____
_____
_____

Encourage yourself:
_____
_____
_____
_____
_____
_____
_____
_____
_____

Date Goal completed:
_____

How will you celebrate?
_____
_____
_____
_____
_____

© Superior Works Publishing 2022

Draw/Plan/Notes:

Date: ___/___/___	Dream/Goal (Write a clear, specific goal):

_____
_____
_____
_____
_____
_____
_____

How is this dream relevant to your life?
_____
_____
_____
_____
_____

Achieve by (Date): ___/___/_____

Track your progress:

Date	Accomplishments

Trust the process…

Reflect (Lessons Learned):
_____
_____
_____
_____
_____
_____
_____
_____

Encourage yourself:
_____
_____
_____
_____
_____
_____
_____
_____

Date Goal completed:
_____

How will you celebrate?
_____
_____
_____
_____
_____

© Superior Works Publishing 2022

Draw/Plan/Notes:

Date: ____/____/____

Dream/Goal (Write a clear, specific goal):
_____
_____
_____
_____
_____
_____
_____

How is this dream relevant to your life?
_____
_____
_____
_____
_____
_____

Achieve by (Date): ____/____/_____

Track your progress:

Date	Accomplishments

Trust the process...

Reflect (Lessons Learned):
_____
_____
_____
_____
_____
_____
_____
_____
_____

Encourage yourself:
_____
_____
_____
_____
_____
_____
_____
_____
_____

Date Goal completed:
_____

How will you celebrate?
_____
_____
_____
_____
_____

© Superior Works Publishing 2022

Draw/Plan/Notes:

Date: ____/____/____

Dream/Goal (Write a clear, specific goal):
_____
_____
_____
_____
_____
_____
_____
_____

How is this dream relevant to your life?
_____
_____
_____
_____
_____
_____

Achieve by (Date): ____/____/_____

Track your progress:

Date	Accomplishments

Trust the process...

Reflect (Lessons Learned):
_____
_____
_____
_____
_____
_____
_____
_____
_____

Encourage yourself:
_____
_____
_____
_____
_____
_____
_____
_____
_____
_____

Date Goal completed:
_____

How will you celebrate?
_____
_____
_____
_____
_____

© Superior Works Publishing 2022

Draw/Plan/Notes:

Date: ____/____/____

Dream/Goal (Write a clear, specific goal):
_____
_____
_____
_____
_____
_____
_____
_____

How is this dream relevant to your life?
_____
_____
_____
_____
_____
_____

Achieve by (Date): ____/____/_____

Track your progress:

Date	Accomplishments

Trust the process...

Reflect (Lessons Learned):
_____
_____
_____
_____
_____
_____
_____
_____
_____
_____

Encourage yourself:
_____
_____
_____
_____
_____
_____
_____
_____
_____
_____
_____
_____

Date Goal completed:
_____

How will you celebrate?
_____
_____
_____
_____
_____

© Superior Works Publishing 2022

Draw/Plan/Notes:

Date:
____/____/____

How is this dream relevant to your life?
_____
_____
_____
_____
_____

Dream/Goal (Write a clear, specific goal):
_____
_____
_____
_____
_____
_____
_____

Achieve by (Date):
____/____/_____

Track your progress:

Date	Accomplishments

Trust the process...

Reflect (Lessons Learned):
_____
_____
_____
_____
_____
_____
_____
_____

Encourage yourself:
_____
_____
_____
_____
_____
_____
_____
_____
_____

Date Goal completed:
_____

How will you celebrate?
_____
_____
_____
_____
_____

© Superior Works Publishing 2022

Draw/Plan/Notes:

Date:
____/____/____

Dream/Goal (Write a clear, specific goal):
_____
_____
_____
_____
_____
_____
_____
_____

How is this dream relevant to your life?
_____
_____
_____
_____
_____

Achieve by (Date):
____/____/_____

Track your progress:

Date	Accomplishments

Trust the process...

Reflect (Lessons Learned):
_____
_____
_____
_____
_____
_____
_____
_____
_____

Encourage yourself:
_____
_____
_____
_____
_____
_____
_____
_____
_____

Date Goal completed:
_____

How will you celebrate?
_____
_____
_____
_____
_____

© Superior Works Publishing 2022

Draw/Plan/Notes:

Date:
____/____/____

Dream/Goal (Write a clear, specific goal):
_____
_____
_____
_____
_____
_____
_____
_____

How is this dream relevant to your life?
_____
_____
_____
_____
_____

Achieve by (Date):
____/____/_____

Track your progress:

Date	Accomplishments

Trust the process…

Reflect (Lessons Learned):
_____
_____
_____
_____
_____
_____
_____
_____

Encourage yourself:
_____
_____
_____
_____
_____
_____
_____
_____
_____

Date Goal completed:
_____

How will you celebrate?
_____
_____
_____
_____

Draw/Plan/Notes:

© Superior Works Publishing 2022

Date: ____/____/____

Dream/Goal (Write a clear, specific goal):
_____
_____
_____
_____
_____
_____
_____

How is this dream relevant to your life?
_____
_____
_____
_____
_____

Achieve by (Date): ____/____/_____

Track your progress:

Date	Accomplishments

Trust the process…

Reflect (Lessons Learned):
_____
_____
_____
_____
_____
_____
_____
_____
_____

Encourage yourself:
_____
_____
_____
_____
_____
_____
_____
_____
_____
_____

Date Goal completed:
_____

How will you celebrate?
_____
_____
_____
_____
_____

© Superior Works Publishing 2022

Draw/Plan/Notes:

Date: ____/____/____

Dream/Goal (Write a clear, specific goal):
_____
_____
_____
_____
_____
_____
_____
_____

How is this dream relevant to your life?
_____
_____
_____
_____
_____

Achieve by (Date): ____/____/_____

Track your progress:

Date	Accomplishments

Trust the process…

Reflect (Lessons Learned):
_____
_____
_____
_____
_____
_____
_____
_____
_____

Encourage yourself:
_____
_____
_____
_____
_____
_____
_____
_____
_____
_____

Date Goal completed:
_____

How will you celebrate?
_____
_____
_____
_____
_____

© Superior Works Publishing 2022

Draw/Plan/Notes:

Date:
___/___/___

Dream/Goal (Write a clear, specific goal):
_____
_____
_____
_____
_____
_____
_____

How is this dream relevant to your life?
_____
_____
_____
_____
_____

Achieve by (Date):
___/___/_____

Track your progress:

Date	Accomplishments

Trust the process...

Reflect (Lessons Learned):
_____
_____
_____
_____
_____
_____
_____
_____
_____

Encourage yourself:
_____
_____
_____
_____
_____
_____
_____
_____
_____

Date Goal completed:
_____

How will you celebrate?
_____
_____
_____
_____
_____

© Superior Works Publishing 2022

Draw/Plan/Notes:

Date:
___/___/___

Dream/Goal (Write a clear, specific goal):
_____
_____
_____
_____
_____
_____
_____

How is this dream relevant to your life?
_____
_____
_____
_____
_____

Achieve by (Date):
___/___/_____

Track your progress:

Date	Accomplishments

Trust the process…

Reflect (Lessons Learned):
_____
_____
_____
_____
_____
_____
_____
_____

Encourage yourself:
_____
_____
_____
_____
_____
_____
_____
_____

Date Goal completed:
_____

How will you celebrate?
_____
_____
_____
_____
_____

© Superior Works Publishing 2022

Draw/Plan/Notes:

Date:
____/____/____

Dream/Goal (Write a clear, specific goal):
_____
_____
_____
_____
_____
_____
_____

How is this dream relevant to your life?
_____
_____
_____
_____
_____

Achieve by (Date):
____/____/_____

Track your progress:

Date	Accomplishments

Trust the process…

Reflect (Lessons Learned):
_____
_____
_____
_____
_____
_____
_____
_____
_____

Encourage yourself:
_____
_____
_____
_____
_____
_____
_____
_____
_____

Date Goal completed:
_____

How will you celebrate?
_____
_____
_____
_____
_____

© Superior Works Publishing 2022

Draw/Plan/Notes:

Date:
____/____/____

How is this dream relevant to your life?
_____
_____
_____
_____
_____

Dream/Goal (Write a clear, specific goal):
_____
_____
_____
_____
_____
_____
_____

Achieve by (Date):
____/____/_____

Track your progress:

Date	Accomplishments

Trust the process...

Reflect (Lessons Learned):
_____
_____
_____
_____
_____
_____
_____
_____
_____

Encourage yourself:
_____
_____
_____
_____
_____
_____
_____
_____
_____

Date Goal completed:
_____

How will you celebrate?
_____
_____
_____
_____
_____

© Superior Works Publishing 2022

Draw/Plan/Notes:

Date: ____/____/____

Dream/Goal (Write a clear, specific goal):
_____
_____
_____
_____
_____
_____
_____
_____

How is this dream relevant to your life?
_____
_____
_____
_____
_____
_____

Achieve by (Date): ____/____/_____

Track your progress:

Date	Accomplishments

Trust the process…

Reflect (Lessons Learned):
_____
_____
_____
_____
_____
_____
_____
_____
_____

Encourage yourself:
_____
_____
_____
_____
_____
_____
_____
_____
_____
_____

Date Goal completed:
_____

How will you celebrate?
_____
_____
_____
_____
_____

© Superior Works Publishing 2022

Draw/Plan/Notes:

 www.ingramcontent.com/pod-product-compliance
Lightning Source LLC
Chambersburg PA
CBHW081708100526
44590CB00022B/3699